Poetry of Love

Rhymes and Reason

"Come Now, Let us Reason..."
(Isaiah 1:18)

SHELDINE ALTIDOR

Copyright © 2010 by Sheldine Altidor.

ISBN: Hardcover   978-1-4500-1985-9
          Softcover   978-1-4500-0907-2
          eBook   978-1-4500-0908-9

All rights reserved. No part of this book may be reproduced or transmitted in any form or by any means, electronic or mechanical, including photocopying, recording, or by any information storage and retrieval system, without permission in writing from the copyright owner.

Print information available on the last page.

Rev. date: 01/29/2016

To order additional copies of this book, contact:
Xlibris
1-888-795-4274
www.Xlibris.com
Orders@Xlibris.com
566038

Table of Contents

Can I Get A Witness? 5
Quote From Ellen G. White 13

Family Poems 15
   Family 17
   Mothers 20
   Fathers 22
   The Walk of Experience 24
   For Women's Ministry 26
   One Body, One Mind, One Purpose 28

Cultural Poems 31
   Remembrance (Black History Month) 33
   Diversity is Beauty 35

Conscientious Poems 37
   Amazing Grace 39
   Refocused 40
   Reality Check 42
   Let's Give Back 43
   The Wakening 44
   Lack of Communication 45
   Re-birth 46
   Nature Speaks Louder Than Words 49

Prophetic Poem 51
   Biblical Prophecy 53

Merciful Poems 55
   The Rock 57
   Emmanuel 59

Victory Poems 61
   Soldiers of Christ 63
   Spirit of Rejoice 65
   Eye of the Storm 66

Maranatha Poem 69
    The Grand Appearance 71

The Agapé Soup 72

The 7 Loving Promises of God 74

Appeal 76

Acknowledgment 77

Sermon Notes 78

CAN I GET A WITNESS?

My Testimony

Revelation 12:11 "And they overcame him by the blood of the Lamb, and by the word of their testimony; . . ."

Growing up in a middle class family, raised by a strong, sacrificial hard working mother of who definitely has the kind of faith that can move mountains. I guess I could say that I was a miracle baby, for I was the third cesarian baby out of whom the doctors declare that my mother will not be able to have anymore after having the first two. The words uttered by these doctors sounded like as though it was impossible for her to give birth. Kind of sounds familiar with the story when Abraham (who by the way was 100 years of age) was in disbelief when God had told him that his wife Sarah will bare a son at the age of 99 years old. You can find this in the book of Genesis 17:17. Due to the fact, that God also has a sense of humour, he then told Abraham for he had laughed at the thought, that you should name your son Isaac (which by interpretation in Hebrew means "laughter" or "he laughs"). This is what faith does. It goes beyond what the human mind can fathom or comprehend (see definition of faith in Hebrews 11:1). It goes beyond, what the eyes can behold or what the ears can bear. It is grasping or taking hold on what is unseen, yet hoping and claiming the results that are bound to happen. It is supernatural and surpasses any amount or weight of visible evidence. The famous cliché "seeing is believing" is not synonymous with faith. The Lord revealed unto my mother, that she will conceive not only another child, but another cesarian girl child and a fourth one after me. I am a living proof of that miracle, and it was only because of the mercies of God, why I am here today.

As a child, I loved to draw especially different faces and shapes of people. I would draw cartoons in comic format, and enjoyed hanging out with friends and family. I was indeed into sports, and my mom used to teach me and my younger brother piano, and we played by ear. My mom had sent me to an elementary school by the name of Sinclair Laird, after graduating from elementary, I was then sent to LaurenHill Academy. These schools were mainly schools which required the wearing of uniforms, for my mom always believed in standard discipline.

During the high school years, was quite interesting, for it was when in the latter part of the high school graduation year, that I had first met the Lord. I had remembered my mom used to tell me since childhood, that it was good for me to attend Church services. By birth, I was a Roman Catholic, but a non practicing one. Of course, me and my little mind, I would say yes and then kind of let it slide by. She would mention to me also the following; "no boys until you finish your high school", that I had promptly took into consideration because, boys or having the mere thought of having a boyfriend would be a distraction and a hindrance to my school work. Do mind you, in terms of religion, I was irreligious and was not spiritual, yet I was very open to new knowledge and truths. I had only attended Church services on special occasions such as Easter, Christmas and Communion. I did not understand the concept of eating the bread or drinking the wine, but I had remembered that the juice was sour and not agreeable to the taste buds.

In terms of my appreciation for music and art, I used to compose hip hop and reggae lyrics and would rap them. I was accustomed and exposed to Caribbean music, and hip hop music since my early childhood, and like a sponge was absorbing the good and bad influences alike, and was exposed to violence and mental abuse. My cousin from Staten Island, New York, had inspired me to compose hip hop and reggae lyrics, he had a gift whereas, if you give him a topic, he will chant or rap on the spot. Therefore, I had performed in high school, and during block parties or barbecue gatherings, I would rap one of the lyrics that I had written. There were local rap groups and young inspired artists that had wanted me to join their group, but somehow I had refused, for I did not felt the need to be part of one.

As every average teenager, all I wanted to do was to experience different things and have fun. I was sent to the Air Cadets along with my younger brother, for three years, and had graduated as a Corporal. We had participated in the Remembrance Day parade, and I was appointed Commander for the flag party. Throughout high school, because I had interest for many things, I had taken the following courses: I.T.T., Art, Drama, Home Economics, Physical Education and Civil Law. Now, being gifted with versatility, it can indeed work with you, and at times against you. Why, I say this because, it can prohibit you from concentrating to the one thing you want to focus on and sticking to it. However, with this versatility, you can enhance in all your gifts and bless those around you.

Therefore, you can imagine what I had enjoyed from taking these courses during my high school years. In I.T.T., I was interested in learning the components of a home and how they were built. In Art, I enjoyed painting, abstract art, anything in art I had appreciate and still do. My grandmother was a painter; my father drew people and designer clothes and was into fashion designing. My mother drew nature and landscaping, my two older brothers drew people and word art. My younger brother drew Japanese style art; ironically today he does graphic designing. In Drama, I used to enjoying acting and taking part in plays and skits. In Civil law, I used to watch from childhood court cases, and in class would play the role of the jury. At times the attorney and had perform cross examinations, and I had remembered as a class, we attended a court hearing just to see what it would be like in reality with real situations and with real people. Of course, these things were not taken as a mere coincidence, for ironically, my great grand uncle, Sir Grantley Adams, was the first premier in Barbados (airport named after him) as well as his son followed in his footsteps. He was once a lawyer as well, and always believed in fighting to relieve the poor and the oppressed. My mom, Joan Adams, was recently, this year, part of a democratic party *Vision Montreal*, and was a member of Tandem Montreal, and had worked and dealt with the public. Last year, I had took a course in Legal Secretarial, I was often asked, "Why don't you become a lawyer?" I had and still have the tendency to ask a lot of questions, and have tendency to conduct a lot of research on things that I hear and absorb. Home Economics was another one of my favorite subjects chosen because, I enjoy cooking, baking, and sewing, and hence, I enjoy domestic duties. One of the experiments exercised was turning a blanket into a pyjama! Physical Education was definitely something enjoyable for it entails the enhancement of physical exercise and physical well being. Overall, I played in a soccer team during elementary years, was involved in Martial Arts, Basketball, Volleyball, Dodge ball, Floor Hockey, Ice Skating, Gymnastics and Touch Football and many more.

Now even though, all of these things were quite fulfilling, it still was not enough. One Friday evening, after having graduated from Laurenhill Academy during the summer, I was bored and wanted to hang out at the Arcades. Upon my return from the Arcades, at the age of 18, I had ran into an old friend, while taking the city bus back home. We were engaged in a conversation, he was with a friend from New Jersey. At the time, I was feeling empty inside even though, I attended numerous parties, went to many hang outs and all of the above, yet it was not still sufficient enough for my hungry soul.

As the bus was heading back to my destination, I had asked, where they were coming from, and he had mentioned that they came from a youth social gathering. Of course, I had to inquire more of what he had meant, so I wanted him to elaborate. He stated that he was coming from Church and that their main discussion was about the Bible. Of course, at that time, I had never read the Bible, except Psalms 23. My friend had sensed the emptiness and yearning through my eyes, and the Lord used him to fulfill the desire to open my mind of curiosity and questionings, he had given me a pamphlet with the Church address. Bear in mind, French was not my first language, and it was a French Church that they had attended. Since attending the youth gatherings, I had to ask my friend (whom I had met in the bus from New Jersey), to translate for me. I was taught about the observance of Sabbath which was on Saturday and not Sunday, and that was foreign to me. I asked, "Wow, there are Church services on Saturday?" I had never heard of this before. I had learned that even the early Christians and Adam and Eve had kept the Sabbath day on a Saturday. Even God Himself had rested on the seventh day. You may find this in the book of Genesis 2:2. I had learned that truthfully there are not 10 recommendations, but 10 commandments (you may find this reference on Exodus 20:8-11). I had learned that Saturday is not only for the Jews but for the Gentiles alike. Logically, if the Sabbath were only for the Jewish nation, and considering that the Sabbath is part of the commandment, the 4th commandment, then lying, stealing, not worshipping other gods, no adultery is only for the Jews. That within itself is contrary to the God of all creation. I had also learned about the dress reform, how a woman ought to dress in order to glorify God. That is a long topic within itself, so I will spare you the details for now. The three Angel's message was also brought to my attention, and you can find this in Revelation 14:6-12. I had learned the truth about righteousness by faith, which indicates that we cannot be self righteous neither our works can bring us to heaven. That is the denial of self and allowing Jesus to reign, where He through us can make us perfect. For in Matthew 5:48, the Lord requires us to be perfect as our Father in heaven is perfect. God would not command us something that is beyond impossible, for what is impossible for man is possible for God (Matthew 19:26).

I had learned about the health message and the importance of our bodies as the temple of God that we must glorify Him in our bodies. I learned the importance of not wearing jewellery because it had led the Israelites to idolatry (see reference in Ezekiel 11:18 and many other texts support this). The sanctuary message and what the Bible says about these things, for salvation is found through the sanctuary, Jesus Himself is the High Priest in heaven interceding in our behalf after His resurrection (see Hebrews 6:13-7:28). I was used to having only the New Testament along with Psalms and Proverbs. I had seen the logic of the importance of having the Old and New Testament, because it is like taking half a novel, it would be incomplete. I learned that the Bible needs to have a beginning in order to understand the current and the future. I had seen that the contents of the Bible are divided into four categories : historical, poetic, epistle or letters and prophetic. With keen interest, I was hungry for more and my searching for truth grew deeper. The Lord knew this and this was why He had led me to these people and to this Church. Six months later, I had gotten baptized, in the Seventh Day Adventist Church. But it does not stop there, I had done it partially out of fear, and partially I wanted to surrender and experience Jesus for myself. By attending services regularly on a weekly basis, my knowledge and comprehension of French had rapidly increased! I was offered a French Bible and a French hymnal, and instead of receiving translations for every sermon, the Lord used me to translate to other visitors who did not spoke a word of French.

As my experience in the Lord went on, I still had a struggle with worldly music and worldly associations. I had then realized that I had not fully surrendered to Jesus. I had learned that God is not a mean dictatorial God who sits on the throne, and zaps you out of existence if you do not give your life to Him or once you fall and make mistakes. In Lamentations 3:22, Jeremiah, the weeping prophet was weeping because the Israelites had not obeyed the voice of the Lord, and are suffering the consequences of it. In verse 22, he indicates that it is because of God's mercy that we are not consumed. He had acknowledged this. I had learned that God is the God of second chances, and promises that He is able to keep us from falling; you may find this in Jude 24.

In the summer of 2006, I was invited to a weekend Youth Retreat, entitled "True Conversion", and was led by a former rapper himself by the name of Marquis Johns. Again, I had seen the Lord hearing my inner sighs, when I was dissatisfied with my walk with Him. With eagerness to improve my relationship with Him, happily I had attended this retreat. It was a time and moment for me to look and search my heart deeply, and to see where I am lacking and where I needed to improve. Times were difficult growing up, but despite of the obstacles, hardships, and circumstances, the Lord had always continued walking with me and holding my hand every step of the way. I was still a spiritual babe in His sight in need of making the transition from milk doctrine to solid food doctrine. I was used to hearing basic, surfacing messages that related to God's love and His grace and surfaces were touched regarding health, sanctuary message, and music. But, the Lord saw it fit for me to start chewing on these topics through His word on a deeper level and on a persistent basis. Jesus saw that I was His sheep that was scattered, and lost. I had noticed that I can still be physically in the Church on a weekly basis, still had took part in door to door Evangelism and other activities in the Church. Always had made sure I was in the front seat of the pews in order to captivate every word of the sermons preached. Had attended every seminar you can think of whether rain, sunshine or storm, had braved the weather in order to attend these seminars. Even had took part in many Christian concerts, was involved in the Choir, yet still I was lost. So the Faithful Shepherd had compassion on me and placed me as His sheep on His shoulder, until I was safely back in the fold. I was physically in Church, for I had never left the Church, yet I was mentally and spiritually elsewhere.

Finally, after attending the youth retreat, perception of music had changed gradually. I had still held on to rap music, rap Gospel music and other cultural things that was a hindrance between me and my Lord. I was not able to distinguish between the sacred things and the profane. I had then attended a special seminar on music once more led by Marquis Johns, who is currently a minister for the Lord in the Seventh Day Adventist Church. After attending the music seminar, reality had sunk in. The music that I was holding on to, did not glorify God. I had learned that even the music we listen to can either invite His presence or invite the presence of demons. If we look around and see how music has affected a lot of the young minds today, we can see its hypnotic and detrimental effect. On the other hand, there are positive attributes to sweet, melodic and heavenly music which is therapeutic for the mind, body and soul. As well, there are types of music that can be disruptive and produce opposite effects. It is God's desire for us to be prosperous and in good health (see 3 John 1:2). The reality is that there was and still is a great controversy that had started in heaven between God the Creator, and Lucifer his adversary, the creation.

At the end of the seminar in August 2006, I had decided to get re-baptized and got rid of all the music that was a stumbling block between the Lord and I. I had then discovered Jesus Christ and had gotten into a deeper relationship with Him. He had changed my taste buds in terms of what style of music I used to admire. The things I used to love, I now hate, and the things I had used to hate, I now love and appreciate.

The Christian walk is indeed a journey and still is and will be until Jesus returns. There are mountains and valleys, but fortunately, the great Shepherd does not leave us alone, He carries us all the way through. Yes, in reality there are and will be hardships, but I am thankful knowing that I serve a risen Saviour who lives and who has redeemed me by His blood. Therefore, because He lives, I can face tomorrow. He has inspired me to do many things for Him so that His name and His name alone may be glorified. The true Author of this book is Jesus Christ, and I am simply His messenger. My love for the Lord has increased and will be increasing by His grace, and I know He loves me and I know He loves you too. For He had shown me the difference between mental and heart religion. He has taught me through the writings of Ellen G. White, of whom we believe as God's ordained Prophetess, for the testimony of Christ is the Spirit of Prophecy (see Revelation 19:10). Prophets were needed in the time of when the Israelites as well as the Gentiles had always gone astray from God's Word. They are like the magnifying glass of God's word. Like the moon (the lesser light) is dependant from the Sun (the greater light) (see Genesis 1:16). The Lord will definitely continue in me, with what He once started!

It is indeed a joy not only to be loved and appreciated by my family, but also to be apart of the spiritual family, for the Lord has granted me a whole new world in Him. I am experiencing the joy of what it means to be a new creature, forgetting things which are past and pressing on towards the mark and to behold the prize which is non perishable. I am experiencing the joy of telling others the love of Christ and His salvation towards us as His mankind, and that by His grace, I shall see Him one day face to face, along with friends and family in His glorious and triumphant return! It will be a great reunion, nothing compared to the 10 year high school reunion here, but I am talking about the kind of reunion that took place thousands and thousands of years ago. From the faithful pioneers during the time of Adam until the future people of God who had lived faithfully in Him near the closing of probation. Rest assured, we will all have a lot of things to say and ask when our Lord Jesus Christ returns and will definitely have a lot of catching up to do!

Hopefully, by His grace, we shall meet the Lord when He returns, and dwell with Him forevermore! I am thankful for the reassuring promise that He will wipe every tear from our eyes that there shall be no more death, nor sorrow, for the former things will pass away! You may find this sweet promise in Revelation 21:3, 4. By His grace, I shall see the King. My prayer is when we enter into a new vivifying relationship with Him; we shall indeed see the King, who has made it all possible.

May God bless and be with us all.

QUOTE FROM ELLEN G. WHITE

The Lord wants all to understand His providential dealings now, just now, in the time in which we live. There must be no long discussions presenting new theories in regard to prophecies which God has already made plain. Now the great work from which the mind should not be diverted is the consideration of our personal safety in the sight of God. Are our feet on the Rock of ages? Are we hiding ourselves in our only Refuge? The storm is coming, relentless in its fury. Are we prepared to meet it? Are we one with Christ as He is one with the Father? Are we heirs of God, and joint heirs with Christ? Are we working in co-partnership with Christ?

Already kingdom is rising against kingdom. There is not now a determined engagement. As yet the four winds are held until the servants of our God shall be sealed in their foreheads. Then the power of earth will marshal their forces for the last great battle. How carefully should we improve the little remaining period of our probation. How earnestly should we examine ourselves. How [earnestly] should we consider and cherish faith before God. How [earnestly] should we eat the flesh and drink the blood of the Son of God, that is, carefully study the Word, eat it, digest it, make it a part of our being. We are to live the Word, not keep it apart from our lives. The character of Christ is to be our individual character. We are to be transformed by the renewing of our hearts. Here is our only safety. Nothing can prevail to separate a living Christian from God.

It is discipline of spirit, cleanness of heart and thought, that is wanted. This is of more value than brilliant talent, than tact or knowledge. An ordinary mind, trained to obey a "Thus saith the Lord," is better qualified for the Lord's work in all circumstances than are those who have capabilities and do not employ them rightly. Christ is truth. He is the truth of ancient types. He is the truth because he is the fulfillment of ancient prophecies.

Men may suppose that they shall be saved, and yet they perish. They may take pride in great knowledge in worldly things, but if they have not a knowledge of the true God, of Christ, the Way, the Truth, the Life, they are deplorably ignorant, and their acquired knowledge will perish with them. Secular knowledge is power; but the knowledge of the Word, which has a transforming power upon the human mind, is imperishable; it is knowledge sanctified. It is life and peace and joy forever. The deeper knowledge men may have, sanctified wholly unto God, the more they will appreciate the value of Jesus Christ.—Ms 32a, 1896. Ellen G. White Estate Washington, D.C. Nov. 5, 1987. Entire Manuscript.

Family Poems

"Honour your father and your mother, as the LORD your God has commanded you, so that you may live long and that it may go well with you in the land the LORD your God is giving you." (Deuteronomy 5:16 NIV)

FAMILY

THERE WAS A MAN TALKING WITH A GROUP OF PEOPLE
SHARING WHAT WAS DEAR TO HIS HEART
IN AMAZEMENT WHILE THEY ALL GATHERED
TO LISTEN HE SAID, "HMMM . . . WHERE SHOULD I START?"

"TODAY EVERYONE I WILL TALK ABOUT
SOMETHING THAT IS VERY IMPORTANT
IT IS SOMETHING THAT I WISH FOR YOU ALL TO THINK ABOUT
THAT YOU SHOULD CHERISH MOMENT BY MOMENT"

I WILL TALK TO YOU ABOUT FAMILY
I WILL TELL YOU WHAT EACH LETTER MEANS
THE AGE GROUP OF THE PEOPLE LISTENING
WERE ADULTS, CHILDREN AND LATE TEENS

F IS FOR FELLOWSHIPPING WITH THOSE
WHO YOU CAN RELATE TO
FOR YOU SEE THEM AS YOUR BRETHREN
TO STAND BY THEM NO MATTER WHAT THEY'RE GOING THROUGH

A IS FOR APPRECIATING
FOR ONE ANOTHERS TIME AND COMPANY
LIFTING EACH OTHER UP SO THAT
WE WILL ALWAYS REMAIN HAPPY

M IS FOR MERCY AND MAKING SURE YOUR BRETHREN
DO NOT FALL INTO A PIT
TO TELL THEM TO DO THE RIGHT THING
TO REMIND THEM THAT THEY SHOULD NEVER QUIT

I IS FOR IMMERSING YOUR BROTHERLY LOVE
WITH TENDER LOVING CARE
SO THAT THE WORLD SEES TRUE LOVE
THAT IT SHOULD BE SPREAD EVERYWHERE

L IS FOR LEADING OTHERS TO KNOW
WHAT FAMILY IS ALL ABOUT
THAT IT'S MORE THAN JUST STICKING TOGETHER
FOR WE SHOULD STAY TOGETHER WITHOUT A DOUBT

Y IS FOR YOU AND ME TO REMEMBER
AND TO KEEP IN MIND
THAT WE SHOULD NEVER LEAVE
EACH OTHER BEHIND

AFTER HE HAD FINISHED, ONE OF THEM REPLIED
"WELL, I REALIZE I'M SITTING WITH MY FAMILY NOW
BESIDES MY FAMILY, I NOTICED ALL OF US ARE ONE",
AS THE GENTLEMAN RAISED HIS BROW

HE GAVE THE EXAMPLE OF NOAH AND HIS FAMILY
WHO WERE SAVED FROM THE FLOOD
AND REMEMBERED HOW THEY GOT SAVED,
AND ALSO REMEMBERED JESUS' BLOOD

AS THE MAN ON THE HILL DISMISSED THE ASSEMBLY
AND EVERYONE BID THEIR FAREWELLS AND GOODBYE
HE LOOKED UP TO THE SKY THANKING GOD
A TEAR THEN SHED IN HIS EYE

TILL ONE OF THEM SAID, "WHY ARE YOU CRYING
MY BROTHER?" HE THEN REPLIED,
I WAS TOUCHED BY YOUR STATEMENT ABOUT NOAH
FOR I LOST MY FAMILY IN A TRAGEDY HE CRIED

ANOTHER SAID, BUT WE ARE FAMILY NOW
DON'T WEEP NO MORE, FOR GOD GAVE YOU A NEW FAMILY
SO THEY GAVE EACH OTHER A BIG HUG AND REJOICED
AND THEY WERE IN PERFECT JOY AND HARMONY

MOTHERS

NOTHING BEATS A MOTHER'S TOUCH
ESPECIALLY HER DEEP LOVE FOR A CHILD THAT IS SO MUCH
MORE THAN A CHILD CAN COMPREHEND
ESPECIALLY HER PROTECTION AND HER WARMTH SHE SENDS

HER TEACHINGS AND EXPERIENCE EMBRACES THEIR FUTURE PLANS
BECAUSE SHE KNOWS THAT IT IS OF GOD'S COMMANDS
SHE SMILES AT HER CHILD'S LIFE AHEAD AND ITS DEMANDS
BECAUSE SHE IS CONFIDENT THAT EVERYTHING IS ALWAYS IN GOD'S HAND

A MOTHER IS SOMEONE WE CAN NEVER REPLACE
FOR NO MATTER WHAT SHE WILL ALWAYS REMAIN IN OUR CASE
AND PROTECTS US FOR SHE ACKNOWLEDGES GOD'S GRACE
AND CAN ALWAYS MAKE AN IMPACT AND PUT A SMILE ON OUR FACE

IT IS NOW OUR TURN TO PROTECT OUR MOTHER
BECAUSE SHE IS INDEED LIKE NO OTHER
FOR GOD'S IDEA FOR MANKIND IS INDEED UPRIGHT
TO KNOW WE HAVE A MOTHER WHO IS A REFLECTION OF GOD'S SIGHT

FATHERS

F IS FOR FEAR IN THE LORD AND TO
PUT HIM FIRST BEFORE FAMILY
FOR HE KNOWS THAT GOD WILL WATCH OVER THEM
AND WILL KEEP THEM ON GUARD FROM THE ENEMY

A IS FOR ACKNOWLEDGEMENT
OF HIS FATHERLY DUTIES AND ROLE
BY PROTECTING AND CORRECTING HIS CHILDREN IN THE LORD
FOR UPRIGHT AND DILIGENT HE MUST BE AND A
HUMBLE SOUL

T IS FOR TEACHING AND TRAINING HIS FAMILY
AS CHRIST WERE TO TEACH HIS CONGREGATION
TO PRACTICE AS AN EXAMPLE,
AND WHO IS APT TO LEAD WITH ANTICIPATION

H IS FOR HEAD OF HOUSEHOLD
WITHOUT THINKING HE IS SUPERIOR
AND IS WILLING TO SACRIFICE FOR HIS FAMILY
AND WHO NEVER TREATS HIS OTHER HALF AS INFERIOR

E IS FOR EXCELLENCY AND PERFECTION
IN ALL IN WHICH HE STRIVES FOR
FOR HE KNOWS WITHOUT THIS EFFORT
THAT HE WOULDN'T BE RICH IN SPIRIT, BUT SADLY POOR

R IS FOR RECOGNIZING THAT AS A FATHER AND A MAN
HE REALIZES HIS DAILY NEED OF THE HEAVENLY FATHER
FOR HE KNOWS BY SUBMITTING HIMSELF TO GOD
HE WILL REMAIN A PERFECT ROLE MODEL LIKE NO OTHER

Based on Proverbs 17:6; Proverbs 19:26; Proverbs 23:22

THE WALK OF EXPERIENCE

THEY WALK WITH WISDOM
AND ANTICIPATE PROSPERITY
SURVIVORS OF FREEDOM
AND FIGHTERS OF UNITY

THEY WALK WITH KNOWLEDGE
AND ANTICIPATE INSTRUCTION
SURVIVORS OF FREEDOM SPEECH
AND TEACHERS FOR THE YOUNGER GENERATION

THEY WALK WITH INSPIRATION
AND ANTICIPATE THE OUTCOME
SURVIVORS OF MAKING CHANGES
AND COMFORTERS FOR THE LONESOME

THEY WALK WITH EXPERIENCE
AND ANTICIPATE OF THINGS ANEW
SURVIVORS OF INHERITANCE
AND THEY HOLD ON TO WHAT IS TRUE

THEY WALK WITH FEAR IN THE LORD
AND ANTICIPATE CHRIST'S RETURN
SURVIVORS OF SPIRITUAL BATTLES
FROM THEIR EXAMPLES WE CAN LEARN

THEY WALK AS SENIOR CITIZENS
AND ANTICIPATE TO HOLD OUR HAND
SURVIVORS SO THAT THE YOUTH
MAY FOLLOW LIKEWISE IN GOD'S COMMAND

LET US ALL HONOUR THE SENIORS
FOR ALL ARE OUR PHYSICAL OR SPIRITUAL PARENTS
AND CHERISH THEIR GODLY EXAMPLES
EACH MOMENT BY MOMENT

FOR WOMEN'S MINISTRY

SHE LOVES TO SERVE TO WHOM WE PRAISE
SHE ENJOYS ITS FULFILLMENT
IN ALL HER DAYS

SHE MAINTAINS HER COMMITMENT TO WHOM WE FOLLOW
SHE SLACKS NOT IN HER DUTIES
AND NEVER WORRIES FOR TOMORROW

SHE FEEDS THE POOR WITH LOVE AND JOY
SHE DOESN'T BOAST IN HER WORKS
FOR SHE IS WHOM THE LORD DID EMPLOY

SHE SEEKS TO ALL WHOSE HEARTS ARE WEARY
SHE TAKES PLEASURE IN CARING
TO WHOM HE HAS CALLED FOR ALL, TO LIVE MERRY

SHE PREPARES DAILY TO LIVE UPRIGHT
WHILE SHE WORKS AMONGST ALL
AND FOR WHOM WHO IS THE TRUTH AND THE LIGHT

SHE KNOWS HER LIMITS AND REMAINS TEMPERATE
SUSTAINS WHAT IS FRUITFUL
AND ALWAYS STRIVES FOR THE ULTIMATE

SHE CANNOT REMAIN SILENT, AND IS EAGER TO VOICE
EVEN THOUGH SHE KNOWS THAT THE LORD
LEAVES US WITH FREEDOM AND CHOICE

THESE ARE THE WOMEN OF GOD AND MINISTRY
FOR HER FAITH AND WORKS WILL BE ANOTHER PAGE
IN THE BOOK OF LIFE'S HISTORY

ONE BODY, ONE MIND, ONE PURPOSE

ONE BODY NEEDS ONE HEAD TO GUIDE
BUT INSTEAD, WE FIGHT AND CHOOSE TO DIVIDE
DON'T REALIZE WE ARE BRAIN DEAD WITH NO HEAD TO CONFIDE
SADLY, THIS MANIFESTATION IS SO OFTEN DENIED

IF YOUR HAND HAS THE POWER TO HEAL WITH A TOUCH
AND YOUR EDIFYING LIPS TO MEND THE WOUNDED HEART AS MUCH
OR YOUR EYES TO FORSEE THE LOST'S FATE IN SUCH
AWAY THAT YOU NEED TO HASTEN BY SALVATION'S CALL IN A RUSH

YOUR FEET WANTS TO MOVE TO A SWIFT URGENCY
FOR YOU SEE IN THE SPIRITUAL RADAR, THAT THIS IS AN EMERGENCY
BUT YOU REALIZE YOUR LIMITATIONS COME INTO REALITY
BECAUSE YOU FORSOOK THE HEAD TO GUIDE INSTANTIOUSLY

SO THE HANDS AND FEET REASONED WITH THE EARS
AS WELL AS THE EYES AND LIPS SUDDENLY UNITY REAPPEARS
SET ASIDE THEIR DIFFERENCES, THEIR DOUBTS AND FEARS
CAME TO A CONCLUSION AND MANIFESTED THEIR SPIRITUAL GEARS

TOGETHER, EACH PART OF THE BODY SEEKED FOR THE HEAD
REALIZED THEIR INSUFFICIENCY AND REALIZED THEIR FAITH WAS DEAD
SEEN THEIR DISFUNCTION, AND WERE EAGER TO MOVE AHEAD
THEY NOTICED THE MULTITUDE OUT THERE NEEDED TO BE FED

THE HEAD IN AWE, AND IN COMPASSION WAS IN VITAL
CONNECTION
TO COOPERATE WITH EACH MEMBER AND IS NOW
READY FOR MISSION
FOR HE SAW THAT EACH MEMBER FINALLY SHARED THE
SAME VISION
TO FULFILL THE WORK SO THAT ALL THINGS WILL BE IN
RESTORATION

NO SPIRITUAL GIFT IS BETTER THAN THE OTHER, FOR
THE SON
OF GOD HAS ASSIGNED EACH OF US WORK TO BE DONE
FIRST CORINTHIANS TWELVE VERSE ONE TO THIRTY ONE
WHEN APPLIED, SOULS WILL BE WON, IN CHRIST, THE
CONQUERING LION

For the message of the cross is foolishness to those who are perishing, but to us who are being saved it is the power of God. *1 Corinthians 1:18*

Cultural Poems

"There is neither Jew nor Greek, slave nor free, male nor female, for you are all one in Christ Jesus." (Galatians 3:28 NIV)

REMEMBRANCE
(BLACK HISTORY MONTH)

REMEMBER YOUR ROOTS
REMEMBER THE DEFEATS AND VICTORY
REMEMBER THE STRUGGLES AND HUMILIATION
CAN'T BEAT SUCH A HISTORY

AS A MINORITY
IN GOD'S EYES WE ARE THE MAJORITY
BECAUSE QUANTITY DOES NOT COUNT
BUT OUR QUALITY

EQUALITY IS SOMETHING
WE SHOULD STRIVE FOR DAILY
UNITY IS SOMETHING
WE MUST HUNGER AS QUICKLY

OUR DREAMS SHOULD BE
PUSHED TO THE EXTREME
SKY'S THE LIMIT
SHOULD ALWAYS BE OUR THEME

LET US STOP WASTING ENERGY
ON CARS, DRUGS, SEX AND GUNS
AND SQUASH ALL VANITY
FOR LOOK AT WHAT OUR MUSIC IS DOING TO OUR SONS

SO LET US CONCENTRATE
ON BIGGER AND BETTER THINGS
FOR IT'S NEVER TOO LATE
TO TREAT SISTERS LIKE QUEENS AND BROTHERS LIKE KINGS

WE ARE BLACK AND BEAUTIFUL
WITH THICK LIPS AND THICK HAIR
THICK SKIN, THICK AS BLOOD
AS ONE FAMILY WE MUST CARE

A HAPPY HEART IS A BLESSING
A CONSCIOUS MIND IS A TERRIBLE THING TO WASTE
THE BEST PART OF ALL IS
TO REMEMBER GOD PUT US HERE IN THE FIRST PLACE

SO AS WE OVERCOME THE PRESENT
AND REMINISCING IN OUR PAST
WE SHOULD ALWAYS REMEMBER ONE THING
WE ARE FREE AT LAST

DIVERSITY IS BEAUTY

THERE IS BEAUTY IN DIVERSITY
FROM ST. LUCIA TO HAITI
MARVELOUS MARTINIQUE TO GUADELOUPE
CREOLE IS THEIR SIMILARITY

LET'S NOT FORGET BEAUTIFUL BARBADOS
FOR ITS BLUE WATERS FROM COAST TO COAST
SWEET SAINT VINCENT AND JAMAICA
FOR ITS FOOD AND GREAT HOST

TROPICAL TRINIDAD AND GREAT GUYANA
HOW WE LOVE THEIR ROTI AND SWEET BANANA
MOUTH WATERING SEASONINGS WITH POTATO
TENDER AND SOFT LIKE THE MANNA

LET'S MOVE DOWN TO AFRICA
LIKE GHANA AND LIBERIA
AS WE SAVOUR THEIR UNIQUE HAND DISHES
AND EMBRACE IT WITH GOOD CRITERIA

REMEMBER EUROPE AND LOVELY ITALY
FOR ITS AMAZING PASTA, HAVE MERCY
AND ITS NUMEROUS COUNTS OF FINE CUISINE
ALL THIS FOOD MAKES ME HUNGRY

SEYCHELLES IS KNOWN FOR IS SILVER WHITE SANDS
A NATION FILLED WITH MANY ISLANDS
RECOGNIZED FOR ITS DIVERSITY IN LANGUAGES
ITS FAMOUS RESORT IS THE CORAL STRAND

LET'S REFLECT THE ASIAN NATION
FOR ITS LOVELY ART AND GREAT POPULATION
THE PHILLIPINES WITH ITS FASCINATING LANDSCAPES
WITH ITS MIX OF HISPANIC AND HERITAGE SENSATION

AS WE LIFT UP CANADA AND THE U.S.A.
OUR NATION LAND AND DWELLING STAY
FOR ALL CULTURES COMBINED AS ONE
FOR WITHOUT THEM WHERE'D WE BE TODAY?

YES, DIVERSITY IS TRUE BEAUTY
FOR ALL THINGS ARE MADE BY THE ALMIGHTY
TO TEACH US THAT WE ARE MADE EQUALLY
AND OUR FUTURE HOME IS HEAVEN ETERNALLY

Conscientious Poems

"Now this is our boast: Our conscience testifies that we have conducted ourselves in the world, and especially in our relations with you, in the holiness and sincerity that are from God. We have done so not according to worldly wisdom but according to God's grace." (2 Corinthians 1:12 NIV)

AMAZING GRACE

FATHER I THANK YOU FOR SEARCHING FOR ME
WHILE I WAS SEARCHING FOR YOU
I WAS ONCE LOST BUT NOW FOUND
GIVING YOU PRAISE IS WHAT I WILL DO

NOT AN INCH NOR A POUND, NEITHER DEPTH NOR HEIGHT
WILL YOU EVER LET ME GO
FOR I KNOW I'M IN YOUR HANDS, I SHALL FEEL SECURE
AND I WILL NOT BE LEFT ALONE

IT WAS LIKE I WAS HOMELESS, OUTCASTED, DESPISED
ENTERING YOUR LOVING HOME
THERE IS NO ONE
AS SWEET AS YOU, NOW I HAVE YOU TO CALL MY OWN

OH KINGS OF KINGS
THERE ARE SO MANY THINGS
TO SAY, HOW GREAT YOU TRULY ARE TO ME
FULL OF MERCY
WORTHY AND ALMIGHTY
BEST OF ALL IT'S NOT A TALE BUT A REALITY

WAS ONCE IN THE DARK
NOW I'M IN THE LIGHT
MY FAITH I SHALL INCREASE
BECAUSE OF YOUR LOVE, MY BONDAGED LIFE WILL RELEASE

THANK YOU LORD FOR SEARCHING FOR ME
I ONCE WAS LOST, BUT NOW I'M FOUND
WAS BLIND, BEFORE NOW I SEE
OH HOW SWEET THE SOUND

REFOCUSED

DO WE BELIEVE WE CAN BECOME ALL THINGS?
THROUGH JESUS CHRIST, LORDS OF LORDS AND KING OF KINGS?
AND SOAR ABOVE THE THINGS OF THIS WORLD?
TO PREPARE TO BE CLEANSED FOR NEW BEGINNINGS?

DO WE BELIEVE WE CAN FLEE FROM SIN AS IT COMES OUR WAY?
AND FLEE FROM TEMPTATION FROM ITS PERMANENT STAY?
TO DISREGARD ALL APPEARANCES OF EVIL?
TO CONSECRATE OUR MIND, BODY AND SOUL DAY BY DAY?

DO WE BELIEVE WE CAN BE AT PEACE WITH MANKIND?
TO WEEP WHEN WE HAD CAUSED PAIN, HAD OFFENDED OR HAD LEFT THOSE BEHIND?
TO PRESERVE OUR ENEMIES FROM JUDGMENT AND DESTRUCTION
TO BE READY FOR THE RENEWAL OF OUR HEARTS AND MINDS

DO WE BELIEVE THAT WE CAN IGNORE OUR OWN DESIRE?
TO SEEK GOD FIRST AND TO BE CONSTANTLY ON FIRE?
SO THAT WE CAN SEEK SOULS, TO BE ABOUT OUR FATHER'S BUSINESS
TO ALLOW HIM TO USE US FOR OUR CALLING IS HIGHER

DO WE BELIEVE THAT WE CAN BE PECULIAR AND THAT WE ARE ROYALTY?
TO BE SET APART FROM A WORLD FULL OF CRUELTY?
TO BEAR THE SAME CUP AND CROSS UNTIL THE END?
TO DRINK THE LIVING WATER AND TO DESPISE NOT HIS PROPHECY?

DO WE BELIEVE THAT WE CAN BE SAVED AND CAN BE
  SET FREE?
FROM GUILT AND SHAME, AND FROM SPIRITUAL
  APOSTASY?
TO REMEMBER THAT WE WERE BOUGHT BY HIS BLOOD,
  THAT WE ARE NOT FOR SALE
SO THAT WE CAN REIGN WITH OUR LORD ETERNALLY

DO WE BELIEVE THAT WE ARE PREDESTINED WITH A
  PURPOSE?
TO RAISE ABOVE, TO WHAT IS TO MANY JUST THE
  SURFACE?
YES WE CAN, FOR IN CHRIST ALL THINGS CAN BE
  ACCOMPLISHED
ALSO IN PRAYER, CHILDREN OF GOD, SHOULDN'T THIS
  BE OUR MAIN FOCUS?

REALITY CHECK

IT'S NO SURPRISE THAT WORLDLY PEACE ISN'T GETTING BETTER
FOR CIRCUMSTANCES CHANGE JUST LIKE THE WEATHER
THE MAJORITY HATES TRUE WISDOM, GOD'S HIDDEN TREASURE
PRIDE AND SELF EXALTATION IS PART OF MAN'S PLEASURE

GUESS WHAT WE KNOW THAT THE WORLD CANNOT PROSPER
FOR THE MINDS OF MANY IS CONTRARY TO OUR MASTER
IDOLATRY AND SELF IS THE MAIN CLIMAX OF LIFE'S CHAPTER
GOOD WORKS AND RECOGNITION IS WHAT THEY ARE AFTER

LITTLE DO THEY REALIZE THEIR WICKEDNESS BEYOND MEASURE
PREACHING FOR GLOBAL PEACE, OH HOW CLEVER
FOR TELL ME WHY THEY CANNOT OBTAIN THAT EVER?
BECAUSE THEIR FOLLY CANNOT MATCH GOD'S WISDOM, NO NEVER

GUESS WHAT CHURCH, WE TOO ARE NO DIFFERENT
IF WE PARTAKE IN THEIR ACTION AND SEEK NOT TO REPENT
AND SIDE WITH BABYLON WITH THEIR FLESHY PREDICAMENT
WE TOO WILL DESTROY WHAT WE OUGHT TO REPRESENT

NOW IF WE SIT AND MEDITATE WHY OUR CHURCH IS DIVIDING
AND EXPLAIN WHY AS A REMNANT OUR LOVE ISN'T BINDING
AND WHY OUR PAST MISTAKES KEEPS ON REWINDING
BECAUSE WE ARE KILLING EACH OTHER WITH GOSSIPING AND FAULT FINDING

GUESS WHAT IF WE PLACE OURSELVES IN THE EYES OF GOD
WE WOULD REALIZE AND SEE WHY THE MAJORITY THINKS WE'RE ODD
BECAUSE WE ARE ROYALTY, PECULIAR AND SPARED BY HIS ROD
TRUE PEACE IS JESUS OVER SELF, NOW'S THE TIME TO SHARE HIS LOVE ABROAD

SO BROTHERS AND SISTERS HERE'S A REALITY CHECK FOR ALL WHO SEEK RIGHTEOUSNESS
AND WHO WANT TO MAKE AN IMPACT FOR A WORLD SO HOPELESS
TO CLEAN UP OUR ACT FOR IT IS INDEED A GREAT MESS
FOR WE HAVE THE LORD ON OUR SIDE, WHY SETTLE FOR LESS?

LET'S GIVE BACK

LET'S GIVE BACK
FOR THE LORD IS GOOD
HE GAVE US THE GIFT OF TIME
SO THAT WE USE IT WISELY AS WE SHOULD

LET'S GIVE BACK
FOR THE LORD IS FULL OF MERCY
HE GAVE US THE GIFT OF GRACE
SO THAT WE MAY LIVE OUR LIVES WITH INTEGRITY

LET'S GIVE BACK
FOR THE LORD IS FULL OF KINDNESS
HE GAVE US ALL PLENTY OF SECOND CHANCES
WE OWE IT TO OUR MAJESTY, OUR ROYAL HIGHNESS

LET'S GIVE BACK
FOR THE LORD IS LOVE
HE GAVE HIS ONLY SON FOR US FILTHY RAGS
AND CHRIST IS NOW INTERCEDING ALWAYS FROM ABOVE

LET'S GIVE BACK
FOR THE LORD IS TRUE
HE HAS ALWAYS BEEN FAITHFUL
IN WORD, DEED, AND IN HIS PROMISES TOO

LET'S GIVE BACK
FOR THE LORD IS OUR STRENGTH
HE GIVES US THE POWER WITH THE HOLY SPIRIT
HIS PATIENCE EXCEEDS ANY HEIGHT, WIDTH AND LENGTH

CHURCH, IT IS OUR TURN TO GIVE BACK
WHAT RIGHTFULLY BELONGS TO OUR MASTER
FOR OUR TREASURES ARE STORED UP IN HEAVEN
SO THAT YOU AND ME CAN LIVE HAPPILY EVER AFTER

THE WAKENING

WAKE UP CHILDREN OF ZION
AND LOOK AROUND, FOR YOU SHALL SEE
SPIRITUAL CORRUPTION INTENSIVELY
FOR THEY ONCE KNEW THE LORD ALMIGHTY

LOOK CLOSELY, AND PAY ATTENTION
THE EARTH IS SLOWLY LOSING ITS DIMENSION
YOU CAN FEEL THE DAILY PENETRATION
YOU CAN SENSE THE MANIFESTATION OF ONGOING TENSION

MUST I MENTION, WE MUST MEDITATE, AND ANTICIPATE
TO FLEE THE WAR OF STRIFE AND HATE
DISCARD WHAT THE ENEMY HAS PLACED ON OUR PLATE
EVACUATE, BEFORE IT IS TOO LATE

BUT WAIT, IT'S TIME TO REASON, FOR THIS IS THE SEASON
THE LORD WANTS TO TAKE US BACK TO EDEN
THE HARVEST IS COMING, THE ENEMY SHALL BE BEATEN
WHAT ARE WE WAITING FOR, MAKE YOUR DECISION

NOW LISTEN! IT'S TIME FOR ACTION, AND LET US SPEAK LESS
AND BEHOLD THE GREAT I AM'S RIGHTEOUSNESS
AND FOCUS ON HIS LOVE AND EVERLASTING KINDNESS
FOR SALVATION IS, AN INDIVIDUAL TEST

SO YES, DO YOU WANT TO FORGET HIS WORD?
UNLESS WE WANT TO PERISH HOW ABSURD
HAVEN'T YOU'VE SEEN, HAVEN'T YOU'VE HEARD?
THAT HIS TRUTH SETS US FREE LIKE A BIRD

WAKE UP PEOPLE OF ZION
FOR WE SHALL FLEE FROM THE FURY OF BABYLON
AND IN CHRIST DAILY THE VICTORY IS WON
FOR GOD'S LOVE, WOKE US UP, IN DELIVERING HIS SON

LACK OF COMMUNICATION

LORD, HELP ME FOR I WANT TO TALK TO YOU
BUT, I JUST DON'T KNOW HOW
MY CHILD, ALL YOU HAVE TO DO
IS GO ON YOUR KNEES RIGHT NOW

I KNOW LORD, BUT I HAVE DONE THAT
AND STILL, I SENSE YOU ARE NOT RESPONDING
THAT IS BECAUSE MY DEAR CHILD
SADLY, THERE IS NOT ENOUGH BONDING

WHAT DO YOU MEAN MY LORD?
I TALK TO YOU DAILY AT LEAST MORNING AND NIGHT
I KNOW MY CHILD
BUT THERE IS MORE THAT I REQUIRE OF YOU IN MY SIGHT

PLEASE LORD ENLIGHTEN ME
I THINK WE ARE NOT IN THE SAME PAGE HERE
THAT IS BECAUSE I AM CALLING ONTO YOU
TO EAT OF THIS BREAD I'VE PROVIDED MY BELOVED DEAR

BUT OF COURSE LORD, I DO EAT BREAD
FOR WITHOUT IT I CANNOT LIVE
NOT OF THE PHYSICAL MY CHILD
BUT OF THE SPIRITUAL FOR THIS I AM WILLING TO GIVE

LORD, I AM WILLING TO RECEIVE THIS SPIRITUAL BREAD
FOR I KNOW NOW, WHAT I AM LACKING INDEED
YOU SAID IT, MY BELOVED
FOR YOU HAVE NEGLECTED READING MY WORD, SO THIS
    YOU WILL NEED

FORGIVE ME LORD, FOR I WANT
THIS RELATIONSHIP AND COMMUNICATION TO LAST
SURELY MY CHILD YOU HAVE ALREADY BEEN FORGIVEN
AND WE WILL REFRESH OUR VOW AND FORGET THE PAST

NOW, I ASK OF YOU TO READ MY WORD AND DO THEM DAILY
AND BY THIS, YOU WILL KNOW MY VOICE
YES, MY LORD I WILL NOW COMMIT MYSELF TO READ YOUR WORD
VERY WELL MY CHILD, YOU HAVE MADE A GREAT CHOICE

RE-BIRTH

LORD, IF YOU ONLY KNEW, WHAT I AM GOING THROUGH
FOR EVERYTHING SEEMS CLOUDY IN MY SIGHT
MY CHILD, REMEMBER I CREATED YOU
AND EVEN IN THE MIDST OF CLOUDS, I STILL SHINE BRIGHT

YES, I KNOW I HEAR IT ALL THE TIME
BUT MY LIFE LORD FEELS EMPTY AND SHALLOW
THAT IS BECAUSE MY BELOVED
I'VE HOPED DEEPLY THAT IT IS ME, YOU CHOOSE TO FOLLOW

BUT I'VE TRIED TO FOLLOW YOU
YET I STILL END UP DOING THINGS MY WAY
THAT IS BECAUSE MY DEAR CHILD
YOU ARE NOT WILLING TO TRUST ME AND OBEY

YES, BUT IT IS DIFFICULT TO TRUST YOU
AND TO OBEY YOUR WORD IT IS OUT OF MY REACH
THAT IS BECAUSE YOU DIDN'T LET ME HOLD YOUR HAND
FOR I AM WILLING TO TAKE YOU THROUGH AND I'M
WILLING TO TEACH

IT IS HARD TO KEEP HOLDING ON
FOR I AM NOTHING BUT FLESH AND CARNAL MINDED
MY CHILD DESPITE OF YOUR IMPERFECTION
YOUR PAST DEEDS AND YOUR HISTORY IS NEVER REWINDED

HOW IS THAT WHEN I ENCOUNTER SOME PEOPLE
ON A DAILY BASIS IT IS ALWAYS REMINDED
MY CHILD DO NOT WORRY
MY LOVE FOR YOU COVERS IT ALL, YOU JUST HAVE TO FIND IT

WHERE LORD, CAN I FIND THIS LOVE
IN A WORLD SO EVIL AND HOPELESS?
*EASY MY BELOVED, ALL YOU HAVE TO DO
IS SEEK AFTER MY RIGHTEOUSNESS*

OKAY, WELL I'VE BEEN THERE, AND DONE THAT
AND STILL REPEAT THE SAME MISTAKES
*THAT IS BECAUSE YOU HAVEN'T SURRENDERED YOURSELF
ALL TO ME, THAT, MY BELOVED, IS WHAT ALL IT TAKES*

OH LORD I AM WILLING TO SURRENDER
MYSELF TO YOU BUT WHERE DO I START?
*BELIEVE IN ME, AND FOLLOW MY FOOTSTEPS
AND I WILL GIVE YOU A NEW LIFE AND A NEW HEART*

FOR I SACRIFICED FOR YOU ON CALVARY
I'VE BEEN THROUGH THE STRUGGLES AND CLAIMED THE VICTORY
I TOO FELT, I WAS ALONE IN THE MIDST OF REJECTION, SCORN AND MOCKERY
AND I DID THIS ALL FOR YOU SO THAT WE CAN SPEND TIME FOR ETERNITY

FOR I HAVE THE POWER TO OPERATE YOUR HEART
AND CHANGE YOUR LIFE BEYOND MEASURE
OH THANK YOU LORD FOR BEING SO PATIENT WITH ME
MY BELOVED CHILD, IT IS INDEED MY PLEASURE

I SURRENDER ALL TO YOU LORD DAILY
AND I TRUST YOU WILL CREATE IN ME A NEW BEING
IF YOU ONLY KNEW, HOW LONG I'VE WAITED FOR THIS
MY CHILD FOR YOU ARE IN FOR A SPIRITUAL HEALING!

NATURE SPEAKS LOUDER THAN WORDS

AS THE WIND BLOWS
AND AWAKENS THE FRAGRANCE OF FLOWERS
AS THE CLOUDS JOIN TOGETHER
TO FEED THE GREENERY WITH ITS SHOWERS

SO IS THE COMMISSION
OF EVERY FAITHFUL SEED
TO COOPERATE AND EMBRACE
ALL WHO ARE WEARY AND BRING BLESSINGS INDEED

AS THE WATERFALL IS FOREVER FLOWING
FEEDS THE RIVERS WITH GRACE
STEMMED FROM ROCKY HILLS AND MOUNTAINS
ALL HAD BEEN RIGHTFULLY PUT INTO PLACE

SO ARE THE MEEK
WITH JOY AND GLADNESS DO THEY FEED
THEIR WORDS WITH HOPE AND LOVE
FOR THEIR HEARTS ARE STEMMED FROM THE LIVING SEED

AS THE SUN SHINES BRIGHT BY DAY
AND THE MOON BRIGHT BY NIGHT
STANDING OUT IN THE MIDST OF DARKNESS
FULFILLING THIS PROPHECY "LET THERE BE LIGHT"

SO ARE THE REMNANT
WHO ARE CALLED BY HIS NAME
TO BE A LIGHT TO THOSE IN DARKNESS
TO PUT OUR ENEMY INTO GUILT AND SHAME

Prophetic Poem

"Then what did you go out to see? A prophet? Yes, I tell you, and more than a prophet. This is the one about whom it is written: I will send my messenger ahead of you, who will prepare your way before you." (Matthew 11: 9,10 NIV)

BIBLICAL PROPHECY

FOUR HUNDRED AND FIFTY SEVEN B.C.
MARKS THE START OF THE 2300 YEAR PROPHECY
AND THE MAIN PURPOSE OF THE SANCTUARY
MEDIA-PERSIA CONQUERED BABYLON ACCORDING TO HISTORY

GREECE CONQUERED PERSIA IN 331 B.C.
THEN CAME ALEXANDER THE GREAT, WAS HE
FOUR PARTS OF THIS EMPIRE DIVIDED EVENLY
THIS ALL TOOK PLACE AFTER HIS DEATH DECREE

EVENTUALLY, THE ROMAN EMPIRE IN POWER
EACH KINGDOM DID THEY DESTROY AND DEVOUR
THIS TAKES US BACK TO THE BABEL TOUR
FOR THEY HUNGERED FOR DOMINION BUT WILL SOON GO SOUR

NOW IN THE 70 WEEKS OF THE 2300 DAYS
THE LORD INDEED, HAS HIS EXCELLENT WAYS
TO KEEP THE ISRAELITES FROM GOING ASTRAY
DOESN'T THAT SEEM LIKE US TODAY?

A YEAR IS A DAY, AND A DAY IS A YEAR
TO THOSE WHO HAVE AN EAR, LET HIM HEAR
FOR THE TIME IS IN HASTE AND THE TIME IS NEAR
THAT THE ONE AND ONLY MESSIAH WILL SOON APPEAR

WITHIN THE 69 WEEKS, JERUSALEM IN RESTORATION
27 A.D. BAPTISM WAS CHRIST'S PREPARATION
THREE IN A HALF YEARS LATER HIS TERMINATION
34 A.D. STEPHEN'S ASSASSINATION

ISRAEL'S OPPORTUNITY AS HIS ONLY PEOPLE IN EXPIRATION
GENTILES ARE NOW OPEN TO HIS PLAN OF SALVATION
TWENTY-THREE HUNDRED YEARS MINUS 490 YEARS EQUATION
LEAVES WITH 1810 YEARS OF PREPARATION

ADDED TO 34 A.D. IS 1844, NOW CLOSELY PAY ATTENTION
THIS MARKS THE END OF THE PROPHECY RELEVATION
JESUS CLEANSES THE SANCTUARY AND MINISTERS IN HEAVEN
AS OUR HIGH PRIEST, HEBREWS 7 VERSE 27

FROM 457 B.C. TO 1844 A.D.
MARKS THE 2300 YEAR PROPHECY
JESUS IS PREPARING A PLACE FOR YOU AND ME
OUR SALVATION RESTORED, BECAUSE OF HIS MERCY

Merciful Poems

"Go, proclaim this message toward the north: "'Return, faithless Israel,' declares the LORD, 'I will frown on you no longer, for I am merciful,' declares the LORD, 'I will not be angry forever." (Jeremiah 3: 12 NIV)

THE ROCK

LISTEN CHURCH OF GOD
OBEDIENCE IS THE ESSENCE
TO GLORIFY THE LORD
FOR HIS LOVE IS FULL OF EXCELLENCE

OPEN UP YOUR EARS
AND LISTEN TO HIS STILL SMALL VOICE
PREPARE YOUR HEARTS
FOR IN DOING SO, WE WILL MAKE A SOUND CHOICE

GOD DELIBERATELY CREATED
ONE MOUTH AND TWO EARS
SO THAT WE LISTEN TWICE AS MUCH AS SPEECH
FOR THE FOOLISH FORSAKES, AND THE WISE HEARS

LISTEN CAREFULLY CHURCH
FOR THE ALMIGHTY ROCK HAS SPOKEN
IT IS NO LONGER SELF, BUT CHRIST
HIS SALVATION IS SURE, AND A SEALED TOKEN

SPEAK TO THE ROCK
AND LET US GLORIFY HIM NOW
THE CHIEF CORNER STONE PLEADS US TO FOLLOW HIM
FOR HIS WAYS ARE TRUE, AND ONLY HE CAN SHOW US HOW

AS WE SEEK TO STAND ON THIS SOLID ROCK
AND BUILD OURSELVES UPON IT
FOR THE LORD WOULD NEVER BRING US THIS FAR
TO GIVE UP ON US AND QUIT

OBEDIENCE IS THE GREAT RECIPE
AND TRUST IS THE MAIN INGREDIENT
THIS ROCK WILL LEAD US TO OUR BLESSED HOME
FOR THIS IS THE REWARD OF BEING OBEDIENT

LISTEN CHURCH OF GOD
AS WE AWAIT OUR BLESSINGS IN STORE
AND SANCTIFY THE SOLID ROCK
FOR IN HIM, DWELLS LOVE AND PEACE FOREVERMORE

EMMANUEL

THE GREATEST ARTIST OF ALL TIME
DECIDED BEFORE HIS DAY OF REST CREATED MANKIND
IN THE MIDST OF EDEN TO HAVE HIS DWELLING PLACE
TO MARVEL OUR FIRST PARENTS FACE TO FACE

NOT CONTENT ENOUGH TO TAKE HEED IN HIS COMMAND
CURIOUS AND CONFUSED THEY NOW CURSED THE FRUIT OF THEIR LAND
GOD'S HAND STILL STRETCHED FORTH WITH TENDER MERCY
DEMANDED THEM TO MULTIPLY FOR HE KNEW HE WILL FIND HIS FAITHFUL SEED

THIS SEED THEN MULTIPLIES FROM GENERATION TO GENERATION
PREPARING CONSTANTLY A HABITATION FOR RESTORATION
SO THAT HIS PEOPLE CAN REMAIN IN HIM CONSTANTLY
AND TO BE SANCTIFIED, EDIFIED AND PURIFIED DAILY

TAUGHT HIS PEOPLE TO PREPARE HIM A DWELLING PLACE
THE ALTAR OF BURNT OFFERINGS FOR THE CLEANSING EACH OF CASE
THE LAVER WAS USED SO THAT EACH BE REBORN
A FRESH NEW START FOR THE IGNORANT AND STUBBORN

AS WE ENTER THE HOLY PLACE, THE TABLE OF SHEWBREAD
OUR DAILY BREAD JESUS WHO WAS RAISED FROM THE DEAD
BEHOLD THE SEVEN BRANCH CANDLESTICKS AND ITS SUPPLY OF OIL
SHINING AS THE CANDLESTICKS WITH THE OIL OF THE SPIRIT, EVER SO LOYAL

AS WE WALK THROUGH THE DWELLING PLACE YOU SEE THE ALTER OF INCENSE
SWEET AROMA IS RAISED, LIKE THE PRAYERS OF THOSE EXEMPT FROM PRETENSE

FOR AS THE PRAYERS ARE LIFTED UP, OUR MAJESTY ABSORBS
FOR THESE PRAYERS ARE APPEALING FROM HEARTS
CLEANSED FROM DISCORD

FINALLY THE MOST HOLY PLACE ACCOMPANIED WITH
THE ARK OF COVENANT
IS SEATED OUR HIGH PRIEST, AND HIS DWELLINGS ARE
PERMANENT
DESPITE OF ONGOING REBELLION, HE HAS A BACK UP PLAN
TO MANIFEST HIMSELF IN THE FLESH IN ORDER TO
RELATE TO MAN

FAITHFUL UNTIL DEATH, HE ENDURED EVEN UNTIL THE CROSS
TO HAVE VICTORY OVER DEATH AND TO RESTORE THE LOST
TO WORK NOW AS OUR OFFICIAL INTERCEDING HIGH PRIEST
FOR ALL NATIONS COMING FROM THE NORTH, SOUTH,
WEST AND EAST!

Victory Poems

"Do you not know that in a race all the runners run, but only one gets the prize? Run in such a way as to get the prize. Everyone who competes in the games goes into strict training. They do it to get a crown that will not last; but we do it to get a crown that will last forever. Therefore I do not run like a man running aimlessly; I do not fight like a man beating the air. No, I beat my body and make it my slave so that after I have preached to others, I myself will not be disqualified for the prize." (1 Corinthians 9:24-27 NIV)

SOLDIERS OF CHRIST

ARM YOURSELF, PREPARE FOR BATTLE
BEHOLD THE ENEMY ATTACKS IN HASTE
GUARD YOURSELF WITH GODLY ARMOR
FOR PROBATION SOON CLOSES, THERE'S NO TIME TO WASTE

GET RID OF THOSE OLD GARMENTS
FOR IT WILL ROT AND RUST AWAY
AND REPLACE IT WITH NEW ARMOUR
AND IT SHALL BE HERE TO STAY

THOUGH SOMETIMES WE CAN BE OUTNUMBERED
AND THE ENEMY ATTACKS OUR WEAK SPOT
YET WE ARE TRIED, BUT NO FORSAKEN
FOR OUR TWO EDGED SWORD IS THE BEST WE GOT

AND THE ENEMY WILL SHOOT HIS WEAPON
IN ALL ANGLES AND DIRECTION
BUT WHEN WE HAVE THE MIGHTY SHIELD
WE KNOW WE HAVE FULL PROTECTION

THOUGH THE ENEMY MAY PLACE
HIDDEN BOMBS AND SNARES, BENEATH OUR FEET
BUT WHEN WE OBSERVE AND WATCH OUR STEP
PEACE SHALL COME TO PASS, THE ENEMY CANNOT BEAT

FINALLY PLACE ON YOUR HELMET
FOR THIS THE ENEMY CAN'T TAKE AWAY
FOR SOON IT SHALL BE REPLACED WITH A CROWN
AND OUR VICTORY WILL SAVE THE DAY

LET'S GO CHRISTIAN SOLDIERS
LETS US NOT FRET, NOT WORRY
FOR THE BATTLE IS NOT OURS, BUT GOD'S
TO HIM ALL POWER AND THE GLORY!

SPIRIT OF REJOICE

WHEN YOUR EXPECTATIONS FAIL YOU
AND YOUR HIGH EFFORTS BECOME EMPTY
YOU FEEL USELESS LIKE A DISPOSABLE ITEM
"REJOICE ALWAYS" SAYS THE LORD ALMIGHTY

WHEN YOU PLACE YOUR BELIEF ON YOUR FRIENDS
EVEN THOSE WHO YOU CONSIDER TRUSTWORTHY
DESPITE OF THIS THEY BREAK YOUR HEART
"REJOICE ALWAYS" SAYS THE LORD ALMIGHTY

WHEN YOU ASK FOR HELP, HEALING OR A WORD OF ADVICE
AND BACKS ARE TURNED INSTANTANIOUSLY
YOUR BACK IS NOW UP AGAINST A WALL
"REJOICE ALWAYS" SAYS THE LORD ALMIGHTY

WHEN YOU'RE HEART HAS BEEN BROKEN
LIKE A SHATTERED GLASS SO REPETITIVELY
AND YOUR SPIRIT IS WILLING TO FORGET, BUT THE FLESH
"REJOICE ALWAYS" SAYS THE LORD ALMIGHTY

WHEN YOU ARE ALWAYS PUTTING AN EFFORT
TO DO WHAT IS RIGHT WITH DIGNITY
AND YOUR VERY OWN DISAPPOINTS YOU WITH UNBELIEF
"REJOICE ALWAYS" SAYS THE LORD ALMIGHTY

WHEN YOU ARE PERSECUTED FOR RIGHTEOUSNESS SAKE
NEGLICTED AND FORSAKEN YOU CRY IN PLEA
YOU FEEL YOU CANNOT BEAR IT ANYMORE
"REJOICE ALWAYS" SAYS THE LORD ALMIGHTY

EYE OF THE STORM

HELP ME O LORD, MY TEMPERATURE IS STARTING TO BOIL
FOR I FEEL TRAPPED IN THIS AWFUL TURMOIL
ANNOINT ME, LORD WITH YOUR PRECIOUS OIL
FOR YOU ARE PEACE, AND YOUR PRESENCE IS ROYAL

GET ME OUT OF THIS TERRIBLE DISASTER
FOR YOU ARE MY GOD AND MY MASTER
YOU ALWAYS SEEM TO SOLVE SOLUTIONS WISER AND FASTER
SEEKING A PLACE OF REFUGE IS WHAT I AM AFTER

HAVE MERCY UPON ME, FOR I TRULY NEED YOU
TO WATCH OVER ME, WHEN I AM GOING THROUGH
OH GUIDE ME WHEN I DON'T KNOW WHAT TO DO
STORM CLOUDS ARE THICKENING IF THEY ONLY KNEW

I CAN CALL ON YOU, LORD, FOR I KNOW YOU ARE ABLE
TO MAKE REALITY FROM WHAT IS TO OTHERS, A FABLE
YOU CAN FIX ANYTHING AND MAKE IT STABLE
YOU KEEP ME STEADY, LIKE THE LEGS OF A TABLE

SO I CRY TO YOU, LORD, COME TO MY RESCUE
FOR I KNOW YOUR NAME IS FAITHFUL AND TRUE
OUT OF EMPTY AND OLD YOU MAKE COMPLETE AND NEW
NOTHING OH LORD IS IMPOSSIBLE FOR YOU

YOU TOLD ME LORD, THAT STORM CLOUDS WILL PASS AWAY
AND PROMISED TO ME THAT THERE WILL BE A BRIGHTER DAY
THEN YOU REMINDED ME THAT I MUST TRUST AND OBEY
YOU EVEN LOVED ME WHEN I HAD GONE ASTRAY

OH FATHER TAKE ME WHERE IT IS COZY AND WARM
SHIELD ME AROUND LIKE A PERFECT DORM
GUESS WHAT, HERE IS SOME NEWS TO INFORM
THAT MY SWEET JESUS IS THE EYE OF THE STORM

Maranatha Poem

"Do not let your hearts be troubled. Trust in God; trust also in Me. In my Father's house are many rooms; if it were not so, I would have told you. I am going there to prepare a place for you. And if I go and prepare a place for you, I will come back and take you to be with me that you also may be where I am." (John 14:1-3 NIV)

THE GRAND APPEARANCE

CALLED AND SET APART FROM A PERISHING WORLD
WHO'S HELD IN CAPTIVITY AND IN CONSTANT TURMOIL
PRE DESTINED TO FOLLOW HIS DIVINE NAME IN ACTION
READY TO BEAR THE SAME YOKE AND DISSATIFICATION

PREPARING TO DRINK THE SAME CUP OF OUR SAVIOUR
EQUIPPING OURSELVES TO ENDURE HIS SAME BEHAVIOUR
HAND IN HAND WALKING THROUGH THE VALLEYS AND MOUNTAINS
STEP BY STEP OVERCOMING, FOR WE HAVE LAID OUR BURDENS

TRIED AND TESTED LIKE OUR PIONEERS HAD MANIFESTED
PURIFIED AND SHINING FOR WE ARE PECULIAR AND BLESSED
SOARING THROUGH THE FIERY FLAMES AND WAVES
RELEASED AND SET FREE FOR THE CHRIST ONLY SAVES

SEALED IN HIS GLORY, NOW WE AWAIT IN ANTICIPATION
ANGELS RUSHED IN EXCITEMENT TO ACCOMPANY OUR ENDURATION
A BEAM OF LIGHT AND A THUNDEROUS SOUND RUMBLES THE EARTH
THE WICKED REALIZED, THIS IS THE CHRIST WHO FIRST APPEARED AT BIRTH

THE WICKED DESTROYED BY HIS GRAND APPEARANCE
FOR THIS IS NO SECRET FOR HIS CHILDREN'S DELIVERANCE
DEAD IN CHRIST ARE AWAKENED FROM THEIR MOMENT OF SLEEP
AND THE ALIVE REMAINING OUR CAUGHT UP AND WILL FOREVER KEEP

OUR LOVE FOR CHRIST, FOR HE HAS KEPT US FIRST
FOR HE LONGS FOR US TO COME, THOSE WHO HUNGER AND THIRST
MY QUESTION IS TO ALL, WHO HAS AN EAR FOR HEARING
WOULD YOU LIKE TO BE READY FOR HIS GRAND APPEARING?

THE AGAPÉ SOUP

The ingredients of love (based on 1 Corinthians 13:4-8)
"4 Love suffers long and is kind; love does not envy; love does not parade itself, is not puffed up; 5 does not behave rudely, does not seek its own, is not provoked, thinks no evil; 6 does not rejoice in iniquity, but rejoices in the truth; 7 bears all things, believes all things, hopes all things, endures all things.
8 Love never fails. But whether there are prophecies, they will fail; whether there are tongues, they will cease; whether there is knowledge, it will vanish away."

- An empty bowl
- An ounce of patience
- A tablespoon of kindness
- A cup of truth
- A cup of hope
- A cup of belief
- A cup of water

INSTRUCTIONS

Take an empty bowl and place it aside. Add an ounce of patience, a table spoon of kindness, mix well. These ingredients are indeed strongholds against envy, boastful attitude, and pride. Patience allows us to await on God working in our lives, and when we begin to understand how He works in our lives, we start to develop the habit of kindness. Once the development of kindness is inhabited it then becomes part of our character. This fighting ingredient also keeps out the diseases of being easily provoked, evil thinking, and iniquity. Thus, this tasty dish will enable you to rejoice in the truth, because the truth sets you free. Wait, almost done, speaking of truth you must add a cup of truth, a cup of hope, and a cup of belief. Without hope and belief which is equivalent to faith, love is incomplete. Last but not least add a cup of the water of Life, who is Jesus Himself. Jesus reassures us that He is the living water, by whom we shall never thirst. John 4:13. Pour this water into preheated pot. Keep in mind, the soup is at its best when it is hot! The Taster Himself will spit it out! (Reference: Revelation 3:16) Perfect! Now it is ready to serve when hot. Remember the empty bowl? Pour the Agapé soup, into this empty bowl. Makes 12 servings. The 12 servings represent the 12 tribes of Judah, and the 12 disciples. This empty bowl represents the empty soul when Jesus is absent from his or her life. Rest assured, once consumed daily, we will sleep like a baby, in other words, we shall find rest for our souls, you may find this reference in Matthew 11:29. This Agapé soup indeed will never fail our appetite, for in Jesus our appetites will be forever filled and nourishing hence, love never fails. Enjoy the soup!

THE 7 LOVING PROMISES OF GOD

Of course, there are more the seven promises of God in His word. However, I would like to point out these 7 verses, that we can believe and claim them for ourselves; knowingly that God will fulfill them!

1. Philippians 4:19 And my God shall supply all your need according to His riches in glory by Christ Jesus.
   The God of heaven will indeed supply all our needs according to His riches. And believe me, the Owner of the universe is richer than any man in this earth!
2. 2 Corinthians 12:9 And He said to me, "My grace is sufficient for you, for My strength is made perfect in weakness." Therefore most gladly I will rather boast in my infirmities, that the power of Christ may rest upon me.
   His grace is indeed sufficient, for when there is a sea of sin there is an ocean of grace, and when there is an ocean of sin, there is a universe of grace!
3. Jude 24 Now to Him who is able to keep you from stumbling, and to present *you* faultless before the presence of His glory with exceeding joy,
   The Lord can help to keep us from falling, instead of allowing us to fall, He is willing to keep us from falling! What a merciful Saviour!
4. John 3:16 For God so loved the world that He gave His only begotten Son, that whoever believes in Him should not perish but have everlasting life.
   Talk about real sacrifice at the expense of His life! Salvation is free and is now available, no money on earth can purchase life!
5. Acts 2:32 This Jesus God has raised up, of which we are all witnesses.
   The One who had been raised from the dead, holds the keys of life and death, because He had conquered death and won the victory, so will all those who believe in Him when He returns.

6. **Romans 8:28** And we know that all things work together for good to those who love God, to those who are the called according to *His* purpose.

    All things work together for our own well being, and no one understands our happiness than our heavenly Father. If parents know what is best for their children, all the more, our Heavenly Parent knows what is best for us.
7. **Mark 16:16** He who believes and is baptized will be saved; but he who does not believe will be condemned.

This indeed is a fulfilling promise! None of these promises are real, unless you believe and claim them! May God bless you.

APPEAL

If you had never experienced a deep and richer experience with Jesus Christ, now is the time. Will you allow Jesus to enter into a relationship with you? If you give Him a chance to lead your life, He will take care of it. He will never lead you wrong, and that is a promise. He is waiting and watching, He is knocking at the door of your heart, will you let Him in? Will you allow Jesus, who is the Author of Love, love you? Jesus says in His word, in John 14:6, "I am the Way, the Truth, and the Life". Because He is the truth, the truth shall set you free (John 8:32). Will you be willing to loose those shackles, once and for all? What is your bondage? Rest assured, Jesus will loose those shackles for you once you let Him in. While He is knocking at the door of your heart, I pray that one day, you will let Him in. If you have already, given your heart to the Lord, now is the time to continue strengthening your relationship with Him. May the Lord keep us, and richly bless us, as we seek Him in love, in Spirit and in truth. The Lord calls us to reason with Him in Isaiah 1:18, where it says:

> "Come now, let us reason together,"
> says the LORD.
> "Though your sins are like scarlet,
> they shall be as white as snow;
> though they are red as crimson,
> they shall be like wool."

This is indeed a promise of love, and a proof of how much God is love.

Now is the season, to reason with the Lord.

May God bless you.

ACKNOWLEDGMENT

I would like to thank all my family, friends, and colleagues for their prayers and support. However, most importantly, I would like to thank my Lord and Saviour, Jesus Christ who had made it all possible.

If you have any questions pertaining to any of the contents aforementioned, I strongly recommend that you study the Bible for yourself, you do not have to take my word for it. The God of love and of reason will definitely help make your paths straight, all your questionings answered, and most importantly your perceptions clear.

"All Scripture is God-breathed and is useful for teaching, rebuking, correcting and training for righteousness" (2 Timothy 3:16NIV)

Blessings.

SERMON NOTES

SERMON NOTES

SERMON NOTES

SERMON NOTES

SERMON NOTES

SERMON NOTES

CPSIA information can be obtained at www.ICGtesting.com
Printed in the USA
LVOW12s0225260216

476753LV00001B/41/P